SandCastle 2

Blends

st

Pam Scheunemann

ABDO
Publishing Company

Published by SandCastle™, an imprint of ABDO Publishing Company, 4940 Viking Drive, Edina, Minnesota 55435.

Printed in the United States.

Cover and interior photo credits: Comstock, Corbis, Eyewire Images, Photodisc, Rubberball Productions

Library of Congress Cataloging-in-Publication Data

Scheunemann, Pam, 1955-
    St / Pam Scheunemann.
      p. cm. -- (Blends)
    Includes index.
    ISBN 1-57765-407-2
    1. Readers (Primary) [1. English language Phonetics.] I. Title. II. Blends (Series)

    PE1119 .S4352 2000
    428.1--dc21
                                                   00-033202

The SandCastle concept, content, and reading method have been reviewed and approved by a national advisory board including literacy specialists, librarians, elementary school teachers, early childhood education professionals, and parents.

Let Us Know

After reading the book, SandCastle would like you to tell us your stories about reading. What is your favorite page? Was there something hard that you needed help with? Share the ups and downs of learning to read. We want to hear from you! To get posted on the Abdo Publishing Company Web site, send us email at:

sandcastle@abdopub.com

About SandCastle™
Nonfiction books for the beginning reader

- Basic concepts of phonics are incorporated with integrated language methods of reading instruction. Most words are short, and phrases, letter sounds, and word sounds are repeated.

- Readability is determined by the number of words in each sentence, the number of characters in each word, and word lists based on curriculum frameworks.

- Full-color photography reinforces word meanings and concepts.

- "Words I Can Read" list at the end of each book teaches basic elements of grammar, helps the reader recognize the words in the text, and builds vocabulary.

- Reading levels are indicated by the number of flags on the castle.

Look for more SandCastle books
in these three reading levels:

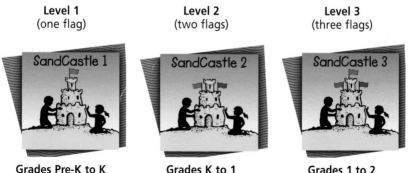

Level 1 (one flag)	Level 2 (two flags)	Level 3 (three flags)
Grades Pre-K to K 5 or fewer words per page	Grades K to 1 5 to 10 words per page	Grades 1 to 2 10 to 15 words per page

Stan and Stacy start their day by having fun.

st

Star steps on the steamy sand by the coast.

7

Steffi has fun when
friends sign her cast.

Steffanie has fun in
her best straw hat.

Stella won the race.

She was first to the stairs.

Stesha likes to push
Stewart down the
street.

Steve and his family stand tall on the big stones.

17

st

Steven and his sister love to hear stories.

st

What are Stone and
his mother staring at?

(nest)

Words I Can Read

Nouns

A noun is a person, place, or thing

cast (KAST) p. 9
coast (KOHST) p. 7
day (DAY) p. 5
family (FAM-uh-lee) p. 17
fun (FUHN) pp. 5, 9, 11
hat (HAT) p. 11

mother (MUTH-ur) p. 21
nest (NEST) p. 21
race (RAYSS) p. 13
sand (SAND) p. 7
sister (SISS-tur) p. 19
street (STREET) p. 15

Plural Nouns

A plural noun is more than one
person, place, or thing

friends (FRENDZ) p. 9
stairs (STAIRZ) p. 13

stones (STOHNZ) p. 17
stories (STOR-eez) p. 19

Proper Nouns

A proper noun is the name
of a person, place, or thing

Stacy (STAYSS-ee) p. 5
Stan (STAN) p. 5
Star (STAR) p. 7
Steffanie (STEF-an-ee)
p. 11

Steffi (STEF-ee) p. 9
Stella (STEL-uh) p. 13
Stesha (STESH-uh)
p. 15
Steve (STEEV) p. 17

22

Steven (STEEV-uhn) p. 19   Stone (STONE) p. 21
Stewart (STOO-art) p. 15

Verbs
A verb is an action or being word

are (AR) p. 21

has (HAZ) pp. 9, 11

having (HAV-ing) p. 5

hear (HIHR) p. 19

likes (LIKESS) p. 15

love (LUHV) p. 19

push (PUSH) p. 15

sign (SINE) p. 9

stand (STAND) p. 17

staring (STAIR-ing) p. 21

start (START) p. 5

steps (STEPZ) p. 7

was (WUHZ) p. 13

won (WUHN) p. 13

Adjectives
An adjective describes something

best (BEST) p. 11

big (BIG) p. 17

first (FURST) p. 13

her (HUR) pp. 9, 11

his (HIZ) pp. 17, 19, 21

steamy (STEEM-ee) p. 7

straw (STRAW) p. 11

their (THAIR) p. 5

J 49007

Match these st Words
to the Pictures

stool

rooster

stump

star